Wetland City

Yongjea John Han

Copyright © 2018 Yongjea John Han

First edition

Designed and Edited by World Letters Press Poetry

All rights reserved. No part of this book may be reproduced or transmitted in any form or by any means, electronic or mechanical, including photocopying, recording, or by any information storage or retrieval system, without the prior written permission of World Letters Press.

ISBN-13: 978-1-7750387-3-3

CONTENTS

PART 1

Salmon 8
Backyard 10
Children 12
Native 13
Waiting 14
The lakeside 15
Sumbisori 16
Wall Paintings 17
The city where the cat disappeared, 18
Wetland City 20
Night Cloud 21
Delay 22
In obscurity 23
At the End 24
Delusion 25
Old wait 26
Zone, John 27
Season 28
Luminous Star 29
Candlelight 31
A Certain Recognition 32
Wall of 11th Street 33
Winter night 34
Way 35
Song of May 37
Gastown 38
Summer in May 1980 40

Some jealousy   41
Some Spring Day   42
Inscription of Unknown Soldier   44
Forest road   45

PART 2

New Harbor   47
Atmospheric Pressure   48
Poetry of an obscure poet   49
Old Drought   50
Life   52
City Bermuda Triangle   53
One Winter Night   54
Children gone to Sea   55
Butterfly Dream   56
Any rainy season   57
Existence   58
Mother   59
Autumn daytime   60
City spring   61
What a journey   63
Reed   64
Orcas   65
City   66
Barren land   67
Past times   68
Night View   69
Puberty   70
What silence   71

Crossing 1   72
Mural of City   73
Crossing 2   74
Way   75
Dove of the city   76
Neon   78
Having met a friend of the poor   79

PART 3

Hometown   81
Some loneliness   82
Plaza   83
The altar   84
Compass   85
Cats on the street   86
Wind   87
Subway Station   88
A buddy   89
Deep   90
Gap   91
I asked on the road.   92
City Aurora   93
Late Fall   94
Trace   95
Empty house   96
Playground   97
Falling Frost   98
Wall Graffiti   99

PART 1

Salmon

There was always trepidation and fear.
in the deep forest,
even the memory stops before time,
it is a place where only the last leaves
are piled up,
the wind is passing.
A moment to stop,
fear is curiosity
thrill has come to enlightenment.
Suddenly,
one of the less grown children came to me.
Every time he passed,
the dry grass was alive
and covered the blue earth.
The saints from Far East,
they pray there.
In the sky,
a meteor began to fall like snow,
everything that lives in tremors and horror
they started dancing there.
The crowd that swam in the distant sea
in one quiet valley of this forest
they will meet their deaths.
We set up a monument for them.
We have to build an inscription.
The boy told me.
They loved the world so much
come to remember,
to those who were at the end of life

we are going to leave curiosity and enlightenment.

Backyard

My childhood is still dreaming
at the bottom of the backyard tree.
When the wreckage of time
is piled up every year
on the traces of my friends,
the children who left home
were not able to grow every year
they would visit the parents' house.
The sad cry of the beast of the night
was heard again,
we embrace the dolls of incomplete
woodcarvings,
I was going on a long trip.
When everything is not alive,
the markings on the tree trunks
became the map of some sad stars,
the stars of the night sky were found
in the backyard of the cabin,
and then,
I had to fall asleep again,
forgetting the dawn coming,
counting the stars.
Such a night will never come again.
I do not want to wake up
sleeping on there
as the leaves fall,
I stopped the wind,
born to cry
I stopped the ear of a doll
made of woodcarving.

Where the wind did not always end,
where I could meet friends if I slept,
when I go there,
I always reach my childhood home.
The place where I became friends of piled stars,
life was not so lonely.
Always visiting there

Children

Before the sun goes down
first we see the moon in the sky.
Like from a certain star
a trail that is not clear
to leave footprints in space
the first time of the night gently decorated.
Our lives would have come so quietly.
Even if the night was coming,
feeling only the dim light
How beautiful is the life to leave?
If we have always walked with you in the light,
if we have just left a trace on the surface of life,
the beauty of the world is that
we do not realize going quietly,
we want to make such a love.
If we look at those who lay there without naming,
not so gorgeous, without embellishment,
we see the simple beauty that is not crowded.
Now the children who make points and make
lines, after that,
considering its depth and color,
down the gray skies
the dim twilight is not scary.

Native

Long ago people who came to this land
from the Arctic's frozen glacier,
on the shaky ground,
the tracks of yesterday
were all on different paths.
There are always many people
who meet in the frozen land that month,
and the illegitimate children
who have forgotten to walk upright,
this year we had to cross the unfrozen sea.
Swimming in the cold deep ocean of the Arctic
when one of the vinyls attached
to the deep eyeball,
such as the seal of the nemesis,
I met and talked to the wacky crowds
who arrived at the old brilliant route.
Wear off the beast's leather,
which seems to break even
in the middle of nowhere
They were predators in a strange country.
Since that day,
no one has stepped on the glaciers of the Arctic
and came to this land.
When they gave up the boundary
and another boundary began to emerge.

Waiting

As long as our bodies
and minds are raised,
hope and love
will be nothing more than the news left
in the lost bag that has been put in a long way.
The road will never be able to absorb
the fog of dawn,
but will leave only a pair of crows
with self-inflicted
self-help
and a lost heart.
We often meet the sun rising
from the wake of the horizon
without realizing that the dawn
is often coming.
We do not blame such people
for being lazy.
We just envied the midday leisure
of making time
along the way slowly,
and we waited for one person
at the bus stop today.
We did not send a letter to meet one,
but the dust was blowing from afar,
and the time that we waited was us.

The lakeside

The wave caused by one of the little pebbles
thrown at the lake shore also tells the story.
The story of a little child, who left an old house,
the faces of those comrades
who had a lot of friendship and love,
touching the glittering starlight on the night
lake, are engraved
on the half-surface of the stone.
while playing house, we made small shelter
with tree branches and straw together.
Our shelter is getting wet in the woods in the
lakeside even if the drizzle is falling,
thinking about the shelter left by the lake,
the breeze passing through the forest,
the cloud flying in the sky,
the small bird flying on the lake, .
where does the children live now and how?
every time I come to this lake,
I pick up a lot of small pebbles
and throw them into the water.
Each time, the faces of my friends on..,

Sumbisori

Woman divers who live in the sea,
breathes out of the sea occasionally to breathe.
Their breathing resembled the whale's breathing.
Human beings were born in the sea.
And the sound of the sea breeze keeps on
following the old fossil memories
like a whale's breathing.
Even in a storm over the sea,
the still calmer sea is more like
the womb of our mother.
Childhood play was an exercise for survival.
My sister and a clear laugh of my comrades
who had gone a long way resembled
the sound of *Sumbisori* breathing to live.
Unfamiliar memories on the wall,
we must swim again in the deep heart of the sea
and make a sound of breath
in this city again to live.
Oh! The most delightful moment of my life!
It's a canvas of my younger days!
As we draw the face of our mother
who has gone into the sea for a long time,
whistle-whistle,
every moment has turned bright,
our lives to leave a small comma (,)
in the world,

Wall Paintings

Like everyone else,
they will grow up in the cradle
with dots, lines and faces.
. , /, □
Our little seeds contain and produce everything.
I met the dots on the street today.
Floating in the air, climbing up the wall,
I met things floating on time like the sparkling
azalea in the spring.
Some go together, others are thin,
and others are thick lines,
and they build houses by tasting each other.
It was a beautiful day.
Some gave the business card.
It was a blank card with no address,
no phone or email.
But I knew immediately who he was.
Look at the memories of the lost cells
and the houses they made.
There was no shape or voice.
Like the people in the degenerated wall
paintings,
I will make a lot of guesses in the face that
will disappear someday
and will live beyond the age.
In what era will I be interpreted?

The city where the cat disappeared,

The city sleeps well beyond midnight.
There is a scent of man
along the narrow alley under the hill.
The street lamps of the electric poles are there
when the light is thinly leaked,
Their new order is established,
buried in an old wall filled with broken
walkways they hunger for the belly of the day
in search of the memory of the horn.
Even the chill of the night wind,
flowing between the fur,
For those who are begging for a day's life
another heartbreaking sore wounds,
they will find nightly cats still castrated
and will spend the night on this street.
They know the old lady who lived in this town.
Every day, on a small wagon,
newspapers were piled up with abandoned faces.
They will spend the night in the wagon.
The news that no one knew
how they lived in this city
until now was their only thing.
They know who went out of the world last night,
parted and loved.
The city did not want a revolution.
They just wanted them to record
and show all the things
that were left behind
without them disappearing.
Here are pieces resembling them.

**Look at those pieces
that are densely packed like stars
in the night sky
and will not be erased forever.**

Wetland City

A group of pink dolphins
who have not returned to the sea
are choosing their last breath
on a strange beachfront.
The brutal May times made the fishermen's
hearts grow harder,
and the moment the last harpoon of hand
pierced its heart,
the petal at the end of the cherry tree that
had been waiting for the summer fell off.
Then the long wandering of people began.
It started hunting people resembling humans
on a wide land rather than in the sea.
They demolished houses built of mossy bricks,
scraped off their tendons and stripped skin,
and began to build other houses on the dunes.
It is to catch a late typhoon after a summer.
They thought that the thin house would prevent
rain and wind.
People swallowed small plastic pieces
floating in the sea with lungs and heart,
and piled them up in perforated stomachs.
They took away memories of primitive.
Little fish came up.
When they started living in a house with
unnamed family.
This is another wetland,
and they will go after the whales
who were about to leave for the sea today.

Night Cloud

I was watching the city covered in darkness.
The cross of a solitary chapel touched
somewhere in the night sky.
In silent ceremony, holy ritual,
I saw a flock walking slowly into the building.
The Lamb of Atonement, the people so called.
I saw a leaf of dandelion through the pavement
block broken on the way.
This city has not forgotten the spring.
The garden of joy collapsed
and a high-rise building was set up
for people to breathe.
The cold chill in the fields was different
from that of the city.
Every day people ran the refugee boat
and crossed the border,
where daily prayers of atonement were lacking.
Today I cut a tree and built a cross.
And digging the land on the beach where
all the sand was washed away, and set it up.
It was always nice to see the night clouds always
forgetting time,
so that no one would be lost in the distance.

Delay

For whatever reason,
those who wait on the platform may have
forgotten their time,
or their loved ones.
Where is the train arriving at that time
without delaying the destination?
We may at some point have to yield to someone
the given time of our lives.
Suddenly we saw twin boys
who died in the arms of his father in TV.
In a time-battling battlefield,
babies were left behind in their unconventional
attitude of ruthless adults.
Their territory was not that wide
enough to be conceived.
We face a storm without warning every day.
And the minaret of the high steeple in the city
grabbed countless hours of floating in it,
and people will either forget time
on an empty platform
where trains do not stand,
or wait for someone who loves it today.

In obscurity

We do not know the depth
and breadth of our thoughts.
Just as you can not see all the world of the ocean.
How many can we count?
With the most limited numbers,
it has become a person
who lives only for survival on a strange star.
There is an unfinished
gray-faced building inside us
that has already begun to be built long ago.
Some people had even failed
to complete the walls,
and others were trying
to break down the old walls
and build new materials again.
But they never finished this long
and arduous task.
Their building became an iconic idol.
I see better races than them.
Our dreams were indistinguishable from reality,
and we had to listen to the cries of a toddler
who failed to live in obscurity.
One must not rely on imagination to know
how deep the depth is.
Get in there.
And touch and feel,
all those moments

At the End

We were not able to sleep almost every day
because of the mass of numbers
and the illusion of the future
that swells up every time we count one by one.
It is called the evolution of time.
Persons will live without emotions,
and only strange types of creatures with
different ideas
and shapes will live on each floor of
a skyscraper built overnight.
They live by trusting in the mass, the imaginary,
and sometimes the natural numbers.
But wherever they are
they will be left with a closed school
where children are not there
and waiting for a train
that will not come anymore.
Those who do not come out of
the numbers eat their mass.
Instead, they might pay a high price.
At every moment we may give up
our childhood dreams with life.
Like counting the number of fallen leaves
and the number of leaves on the tree,
count the number of people
who have left for other places
and those who have left there,
and prepare for the end by enjoying the feast
every day.

Delusion

I saw a scarecrow guarding the fields alone.
Hovering around, sometimes borrowing his
shoulders, he took them with a small bird
that flies, a spiritless gesture.
They resembled those left
behind on the outskirts of life.
Visitors to fill the thirst of the soul
have not arrived yet.
For them, the wisdom to drive out
the birds was just the practice of silence
and the field through the angel.
There was only a small bagworm moth larva
of last winter
that did not sleep yet.
There was only a struggle of thirst
that could not be a butterfly and thirst
that could not contain a soul.
Oh! Can you always get out of this delusion?
From a distance,
only the static sound of the cargo ship
that is about to leave the harbor is heard.

Old wait

I waited for you today.
I still remember the time
when I came from a distant planet.
The planets of the earth have become a sign
that they will not be lost long after.
I still remember the way I missed the warm
sunshine in the coldness
that I did not know how to laugh
and how to have my tears.
Nobody knows whether
we will be able to shine our hearts forever
and always to be able to walk
without getting lost.
I wonder if I have ever dreamed of a dream
that I had swept the countless stars pouring out
on the beach, what I felt,
what I felt like on a broken old house,
I still could not remember my name, address and place.

Zone, John

We must meet people
who have lost their bodies
and wandered under the street lamps
of the street.
There would have been memories of
him having enjoyed his childhood.
There may have been times when innocent
and clean souls were included.
However,
after the fall of winter, he met the cold weather
and fell on a slightly frozen road.
He had no soul,
and he looked only at the lamppost,
like a man with aphasia who could not
remember happy memories.
He had lost all of his life
as he passed through middle age.
Like the graffiti on the bare wall,
he was still scribbling in the broken heart there.
That night he missed the dreaming star
among the buildings.
He said he waited for the unidentified ones.
On the day when the light will someday,
his painting will also be over.
Until the day that the streetlight lights up its life,

Season

I wanted to have a good laugh
and to meet the same season
as the open hyacinth.
But all that is seen is a horrible grave
that can not look at the face and turn around,
and it starts to meet the frenzy season
when it comes to producing
and nurturing the machine.
You've got a new leaf like a cherry blossom
that just started to fade in the late spring.
But someday it will be time to part with this.
You'll have to go on a trip again that day.
Once you find a road that
you can not come back to,
you are leaving our unwarranted future.
We had seen the storm blowing
on the beach last summer.
It erased all the traces
and even the small grains of the sand breaking
shattered the beach of ruins
where nothing remained,
and your soul,

Luminous Star

Sometimes,
I was sleeping while staring
at the noctilucent stars
on the old wallpaper
and ceiling smudged rainwater
seeped of my childhood.
In a small universe that can only be seen
in my room,
I used to be a little prince and dreamed of
visiting some kind of stars.
At a local stationary store,
holding a space ship in my hand
and riding a kite flying high above the sky,
I'll be waiting for a star now.
The world is not that small.
I am going to find my glittering stars
somewhere with the support of my mother
and friends as the growth progresses as the
world grows taller.
Not too far away,
the Balance is gathering to find places
that make up a small town.
My comrade, let us not get lost in this place.
On the clogged path,
asking where you are heading to
the small bird flying,
then my small room was a beautiful garden.
The blue sea was breathing
and the stars were dreaming my own world.

It's old, but I always feel new
when I look at the space.
I hope that our pure feelings are lost.
We must leave behind the pure wills of
those who remain here,
and the memories we will miss
at some point in the future.
Do not forget that life is so beautiful.
Like a pink cherry blossom
that blooms first in a warm spring without you.

Candlelight

I saw the lights on this street.
I saw the strong light
that did not put out before the wind.
I saw the feast of the lights that wave like waves.
Was there such a time
when it was so beautiful and so dazzling?
See how darkness retreats!
I saw corruption and injustice in the darkness.
They were driven out of this street by lights.
I see an old wound of my mind healed
by the lights.
Have you been to that street?
People who fall down are getting up again.
In the oppression,
I will obey the will of the saints
who remain faithful to keep the light.
When the wall collapses
and the border disappears,
the thrilling tears will be shed together
with the dance.
I will resemble the candle,
and hold it in my chest.
Let's go to the street together
and become a candle of resistance.
The lights that can't extinguish before
(   ),

A Certain Recognition

The appearance of the person
who escaped from
the long tunnel was disgusting.
Blood was flowing from the head
to the toe for a long time
and wearing the stench and the dirty clothes.
What happened in a dark, blocked space?
I have created a number of complex ideas.
He fells silent, tired body and twisting legs,
staggering like a mollusc
which lost sight in the water.
No one approached him
and looked at him from afar
without thinking they would help him.
Some people looked at him and even spit it out.
If they knew who he was, could they?
If it were the same as the amethyst
embedded in the rock,
nobody would have been deceived
by its appearance.
The crowd of this city lives in illusion.
And they finish their life.
We already knew him from the old age,
but our perception was pushing him out.

Wall of 11th Street

The sewer,
the rainwater,
the irresistible impression
and the falling water drop to hell,
the man turned the street corner.
The wall was built in 1945 with red bricks.
The man quietly disappeared
into the drain holes.
Before reaching the ground
and enjoying enough rest.

abyss,

There is no storm in the underground sea.
There, the man will probably
grow into an adult.
No one will predict its appearance.
If you interpret the characters from there,
you can use [ ], { }, () ...
You will find that it was a prison of language.
The man will die there,
become a butterfly on the earth,
and have a strange dream to fly.

Even today,

a small puddle beneath
the wall did not contain rainwater.

Winter night

Which winter night was it?
It was raining all night instead of drifts of snow.
When all the people on the street went back to their spaces,
we saw an old bridge
that had been a shelter for stray little birds,
forgetting time.
Leaves fell and slender willow branches
were soaked in rainwater
and could not win the weight.
We counted the number of winds.

smallandmindfulmemoriesthatcontainonthestreet

I could feel the wind
that moistened the water as much as the number
of the stem. That night was a night for greenhorn
dreamers. They have always loved the streets
from the early morning
again dressed in unconscious words.
This was the garden of the poor and the lonely,
the night of deep hibernation,
the sound of the net.
In the diary of the ugly,
there was always greed, anger, and agitation.
It was a night on the street where nothing could
be done.

Way

Along the unpaved road,
I drove through the darkness
that did not even light.
I could not tell where the end of this street
I was going from the first time
I slowly lighted the starlight floating
in the night sky
and the extraordinarily large
and bright moonlight.
I was alone so suddenly
I was not so glad to hear the news of
those who passed here many years ago
I listened to the old song
from the car radio quietly
and hoped that the end of this road
would one day wait for me.
Did you pass by?
I always know that the roads
you choose will be changed by someone,
the way you go every day,
the way you have to go through
your life once in a while,
sometimes I grow in the pain of life,
Put on a lamp that is not packed,
that the end of my days will be near
on the day of setting the lights.
Return home from the long journey to the
flowing melody
and share your love in this way.
When the dawn brightens,

we see our home far beyond the horizon.
We gather the lights of the streets
and share them with people.
One day, the fog on this road will go to its house,
and the little grass on the road will quietly hide
in the ground and winter.
Now I know this road was so beautiful.

Song of May

Until the night of revolution is over!
Do not stop this song.
Do you remember when you were brilliant?
At that time, the spring breeze grew scattered
 in front of your ornate appearance.
The time of betrayal has passed
in your childhood,
waiting for someone in a jail without a grate.
When I sing a song with a song written by
an obscure pen who has fallen,
I have found friends
and all the meaningless symbols
and languages floating in the air.
One of them approached me
and whispered in whispers.
It was then that life was not a vulgar
feast of snobs.
I watched the starlight floating in the sky
in the distant night
and waited for the signal.
Anyone who will sing any song comes to us now
and waits for us. May is that month.
It is the month
when the revolutionary comrades
who fall down in front of the boy's eyes are
raised again.
This grateless prison is dazzlingly
beautiful and warm.
Young poet!
My friend who will sing us the last song!

Gastown

On that street in Vancouver's Gastown,
you hear the story of how many passers-by are
on the footprints on old red-brick roads.
On top of that, the faces of the people laughing,
crying, getting angry, a series of departures,
the gulls of the harbor,
and the sad history of the Aborigines are
carried to the small beak here.
No one wanted to meet the unconquered land,
those who do not want to yield.
The fog of Gastown was not the fog we had met
in the early dawn forest.
It was moisture mixed with civilized steam.
I become a small lattice.
It will be alone in the lost grid
that can never be matched.
There were also small aboriginal children.
I have become part of all of this,
with the scattering of red bricks
and the combination of the lattices of the owner,
the stories of Gastown,
the elderly people who silently pace
and negotiate puzzles
in front of a small coffee shop
at the end of the street.

I have become part of all of this,

I have become part of all of this,

I have become.........?

Summer in May 1980

That year,
May was as hot as summer heat
and did not rain.
The wildflower also had to endure
the midday day
with the dew of the dawn.
The children could not get out of the house
because of the sunshine,
and sometimes a cat without a master
roamed around the town.
He ruled the village without anyone to meet.
It was the first time that did not rain.
Everyone said that our earth was sick.
But I did not think so.
How can we blame this land?
Everything originated from man:
the fading of wildflowers,
the division of the land in the drought,
and the movement of a cat around a village.
I hear a shell sound from a distance.
On the other side there will be
no innocent people
falling to the ground and dying.
I climbed up the hill and watched
where smoke rises.
The smoke mixed with the heat pouring
from the surface,
and made my sweat flow down my back.

Some jealousy

When I came to know that everything
I had lived was filled with jealousy toward
myself, I was already at the age of seeing
the old age. I could not escape from my regret
that I felt and the sense of betrayal for the past
years that I was throwing stones of jealousy
again for those times. The faintness of the flesh
and its loneliness had always had to fight with
the gaze that stared at me as I alternated with
my feelings of obsession and alienation. Late
night, under the streetlight outside the window,
the sound of the fussing toward the world of a
passerby and the fighting of the countless
shadows of the street poured out anger toward
the darkness with the comfort of the world's
noises that would only disappear for a while.
Suddenly I was thinking that a baby sleeping
quietly in the crossing would have this jealousy.
child! You are the only one who loves the
morning fog and a shade. For you, living
in the world, I want you to live with the lightness
that you can have in your little minds even
before you know the word jealousy.

Some Spring Day

I miss spring rain.
I have not been drinking water
for over 5 months already on the dry land.
The land, which was noisy in winter,
had no seeds.
The crowd of migratory birds
that did not know the name
that had flown from Siberia flew
around the dry sky and made an
unidentified sound because they could not make
a nest here. People persuaded
that they should build more cities.
Their eyes were not eyes for survival.
Their hands were so dry that they could not
hold water, and their
legs were already rooted
and tied to the base of a dead tree.
Dry branches and leaves no longer fall
on the ground
and become old fossils.
Their voices were also
closely packed in the hard tree's shell
and they chased away the little
birds that had flown from
time to time. I will not wait for spring rain
anymore. Even if you can not
drink water, they will walk through
the delusion whilst following the memory
of drinking water in the past hour. Soon the
migratory

birds will stay in the sky and return to Siberia.

Inscription of Unknown Soldier

All living things breathe. I am writing poetry today with red pen on white paper on my desk. I will also exhale only this time. In June, when the potato flower blooms, my little garden will also be white. I stop by for a moment and think about those who left the red footprints. Still here, conflict and war are in progress. Can not you hear that sound? They cross over the sea and fall to the beach one by one with a dulling shout. Writing a poem for them is still breathing on this land. Today I confess in front of unknown warriors. Writing line poetry for them is still breathing here in the inscription that built in front of the graveyard of the old churches. A blue jay flying in a forest sits on the inscription for a long time, and he quietly returns to where he was flying. I now breathe in the inscription. Oh! In a radiant June! My mentor who fell as flowers do in the garden of my country! Companions!

Forest road

When the day comes every day,
early morning and take a walk to find a way
to the forest in the backyard of a small log
cabin. I grabbed the morning dew
and just stretched it
and saw the flowers in there.
Even though I could not remember the names,
I envied their patience and attachment to life
that they were always there in my memories
from the childhood to the present.
I will continue to make a poem of the same day,
and thank you for your day
and remember my life.
The forest is my writing,
and this forest I am walking on is the guide
who told me the way to go
at any moment of my life.
Life was as beautiful as the forest
in the early morning.
When the wind blows,
there is a whispering sound among the twigs
that are shaken and burnt. Listen,
Their stories will be left somewhere on this road,
and all the moments of life
that have passed will come to
those who go to the forest,
just like a bright morning without a cloud.

PART 2

New Harbor

I made a new port every day.
The harbor will not come in.
There was no boat to enter.
No one came to meet us there.
Some said it was really foolish.
Sometimes I found only the sea gulls
who were lost
and they were only looking at the sea
and were sitting on the pillar of the marina.
When I began to get used to solitude,
it was not loneliness which I felt
because I could not meet a person,
but loneliness which I felt
while looking at the boat returning
because I could not find an anchorage place.
Over the sea without waves,
the gray clouds gathered,
and they stayed for a while and disappeared.
The harbor did not believe in weather forecasts.
And I spent the day in awe and fear,
thinking about the size of the harbor,
which should always be built
rather than the size of the ship.
I built a harbor every day
at the shallowest places
where the ship can not come in.

Atmospheric Pressure

Cumulus, cirrus clouds
When the traces fell quietly down on the ground,
the people disappeared
after the horrible smell of their dwellings
in order to erase memories of the old fearsome.
What they had in their minds would have
already known
the breathed beings in this city.
It was like an unshaped entity, always at dawn,
heavily squeezed over the roads with red bricks,
and people overcame last night's dread
and cold, and rose again to pray.
Poor house children
and the elderly made plans for
their uncertainty about the future
and begging for the day by their traces,
and repeatedly erased them in their heads.
By the time the sunset to begin,
people who had forgotten
the way home began gathering one by one.

Poetry of an obscure poet

old bookshelf
take out a poem
by one of the obscure poet
shake off the accumulated dust
and reading
in the middle of a book
faded leaves I saw one.
dried leaves in front of the years
it could be a poem.
if you follow the trail,
the pain of falling leaves,
stories of sad parting from tree
and the poet's poor heart
in the book
all of them.
the poetry has hugged forever.
all that he has endured it.
his words were sore and painful.
it was so beautiful.

Old Drought

It was the worst drought in 30 years.
In the daily news,
the voices of the people waiting
for the rain were reported.
At the bottom of the barren lake was
a grave of dead fish.
Some of the fish's dead bodies
will not be able to leap over the Submerged Weir,
and some fish will die out.
The stone walls and roads of the villages
that have been submerged
a long time are exposed
in the dry river bed.
Still, the remains of a zelkova tree
that had been washed down
by the wind of water remained at the entrance to
the submerged town.
Under the tree, the stones thrown
by the people were piled up,
and they were enduring
the harsh dry rainy season.
I have never seen such a lonely
and desperate scene.
I am having the most difficult drought season
of my life right now.
No one was looking for a village in the riverbed.
The body is lean and the mind is
in the memory of a young day
and faces another season of ruins.
However, the drought will continue in this season.

People who can not die can wander again
on the boundaries of the appointed time.
But no one will come.
Besides the gray fog that will stay in the dawn
for a while,

Life

I saw a tree
that had been thrown away with roots
that had sunk on the surface of waterfront.
When I realized
that there was still a desire for life
and a love for the world.
I knew then.
The roots are not buried in the ground,
but they are sleeping on the surface of the water.
As light dawned on it in the warm spring days,
light leaves began to emerge on its lifeless body.

City Bermuda Triangle

Whenever we come to this street
beyond midnight,
we meet a city where the humid air of
one night weighs heavily.
we meet people like moths who are born
and grew up long after leaving home
and chasing lights.
They were always waiting
for the first bus of dawn,
lying on an empty bench
under the neon sign of the city.
When the bells of the cathedral ringing
the first mass rang from afar,
they unconsciously rose
and headed there for a day's hunger,
not for worship. Among the sickly buildings,
one of the grasses was seated
and waiting for spring.
The pilgrimage marches along the long
and narrow road to find
the fossil of the civilized people
living the noise every day.
It was easy to find an abandoned heart there.
Only crows who did not find the nest that night
in the empty theater seats,
the smell of cigarette smell, and the occasional
homeless shout on there.

One Winter Night

We do not want to spend
the winter in this city.
The fierce blizzard to the flesh
feels unbearably painful.
This winter makes homeless people
lose their way of life.
We still remember the warmth of
a familiar tavern.
Go back to each house one by one
and count the souls
of the remaining people.
The singing of the birds flying
to the far south makes this season unique.
The stories of the old revolution on the streets,
we have to hear sentimental complacency
and tired minds for the children of other
generations.
Where are my comrades?
The snow keeps coming down
without stopping, but the snow falling
on the ground does not melt and piled up,
and our stories are falling apart.
When will our season come here?

Children gone to Sea

Our children went to the sea. When we have not promised to come back, we wait for them at the harbor, as if they had made promises. A yellow ribbon is tied around the railing of an old dock and fluttering like a whistling sound of children. Whenever we called together the names of the children who went to the sea together with their hands gathered together, we would always have an empty spring.
It was a cold country without heat. We saw it in the long procession of the dancing dancers singing the song of love that soothes the soul. We were with the people who prayed to the small fluctuation of the candle which flows down with candles in our hands. The faces of the children were painted on the bottom of the deep sea. Mom, about going home soon. Why do not you put it on top of a bowl of warm rice for me? With my mother's tears, I eat this rice that has not cooled yet and now I am going back to my room and sleep. I am not lonely. Our young souls are so beautiful. I hear the breath of a sea lady. Please do not forget the sound. Someday when we hear all of our stories, I am looking forward to the day when all the children who went to the sea will come back.

Butterfly Dream

I lost it, but I always had hope. And I counted those days with my fingers how much time had passed, but I could not put all of them in ten fingers. I couldn't even put it on my palm. Nevertheless, I appreciated everything. Even the less bare traces that still buried in my body were grateful. I knew that I was born twice. When I was born twice I forgot the past in the shell and looked into my changed inside and saw the desire to embrace. From there I can see a train just off the platform from a long tunnel.

Any rainy season

The terrible rainy season is not over yet. It was hard to breathe on a rainy night. At night, I heard the cry of those who lost their homes in the dirt that washed down from the back of a town. All things living and breathing are hard to endure this season. People looked at the gray sky all the time. Across the gray sky, they looked through the black sky, hoping raising the sunlight. The stepping stones of the creek in front of the village hid deep within swollen streams and people were shouting and throwing rocks, saying that they had to find a way out of the world. The history of exploitation was repeated there. People repeated a kind of retaliation against taking away nothing but every year. Such a terrible rainy season is said to be the first time. Human history began at the end of the Flood. Just as the sea could not fill everything, there were people trying to fill things that would not be filled.

Existence

A small sprout, which may be called a name in the future, is coming out to the world with a small gap in the pebble field, pushing a heavy stone with the lightness of its presence. I want you to be like me. Even today I can not push me out. After the rain, the last floating clouds above the sky just do not spray the last stream of water on the ground, It will roam from the ground to the ground slowly. We do not have the weight that we can not afford. It's just because I have to make decisions in advance of everything. Today, I will have to meet those who woke up from the many sleeps on the sunny street. When I walk around the corner, I imagine a terrible imagination waiting for someone there. The pressure of this city is light. Like the movement of the bird's body living in a small tree bush under the window, My voice among them is only light not enough to endure.

Mother

As I look at the snow cape that
does not melt in the summer,
I look at the woman who endures
the pain of marriage silently
and conceives another life.
Her presence is dignified
and wonderful.
When it was a day of coloring again
on the canvas of life.
I saw our mother
who was waiting for the children
who had left at a long distance.

Autumn daytime

When we look at the flocks of clouds
that are in one place,
we must prepare to leave this long way.
When you look at the stone carvings
on the roadside,
you should pick up
your scattered minds together
and prepare a road that is not lonely.
Look at the beautiful city,
once poor people are now
sharing the joy of harvesting in affluent fields.
I will not forsake anything,
I will take all the grain,
and I will share my joy with you.

It is also very pleasing to see
the cheerful wind that meets in the fields.

I will meet my young
and glad and glorious journey of the old days.
I will decorate a page of an old photo album
that will not throw away any memories
on the table.
When that time comes,
I will recall the time with friends
who have put down all the luggage
and have come back along the way.

City spring

The days of the flowers of the small flowers bed that we planted will someday show the bright faces to those who visit here. Winter in the city will not be so cold. One little boy said. In the morning when the pure children's chattering meets the little flowers and makes them dream about the future, the glitters will meet again and again. Would you like to take a bike ride across the hills of the packed roads to the town? You are not a friend to meet an old photo album anymore. Now I know that this road I walked with you and can not freeze even in winter. The heart is still a warm spring. It is a small seed of a flower. It is the mind of a boy.

Night street

I want to stay away from this night,
which is always on the way
as advertised in the city.
Some start the day on the street at night.
They do not depict the busyness of daytime
and the image of everyday life.
It resembles the way
the cats walk quietly around the corner.
We have to break this night.
Put it in the pocket of an old, long coat,
avoid the night
and avoid the place with a dream of noon.
Look at the people.
Enjoying the darkness is not beautiful.
I should ignore the pressure of the heavy night
and the static sound of the car from afar.
The streets of the night are hungry.
Thirsty.
Even shadows are created there.

What a journey

I am so glad this way to go now.
I am thrilled with this delightful journey
that takes away all the burdens of the mind
and leaves with Him.
I enjoy sitting waiting on
the promised train station platform.
Soon as the train arrives at the right time,
I will meet people with neat outfits.
I will talk about my wishes
for the future all the time
while I'm going to my destination.
I know now that my life is like
that of the railroad tracks.
People!
As always, you have to meet a friend
before you go on a trip.
We should have such a friendly friend
who will not be burdened with all our burdens.
I will tell them.
I am here with my friend,
and on a beautiful day
let's wait for the train to arrive at the station
with a light heart.

Reed

The land where the reeds grow is not always dry.
When the wind pushes the reed lightly,
the wind will spread through the reed leaves
and the fond memories of those who
can be forgotten as they gaze at
the wings of the bald eagle fly above the sky.
It is probably because of the hidden fossils of
my childhood that the small movements of
the old reeds seem to be small vibrations in a city
that is alive and returning one by one
when everything is stopped along
the gray light fence.
The people on the streets
where the rain falls are shaking each other.
Perhaps their land was not dried.

Orcas

I saw Orcas of the sea.
Reflected in the moonlight, the heavy backstreet was as clear as moonlight. People do not know their reality. I only knew that beautiful, white painted spots were gentle and gentle sea gentlemen. But for them, they knew that the sea stood on the high seats of predators. When I saw their appearance, they are clear and horrible traces behind the gloriously disguised figure. As I was living a day, I knew that all living creatures showed their vigor and ruthlessness for survival. Among the colorful buildings of the city are orcas. When the lights are shining on top of each other, the appearance of the lost ones comes to mind. It is the night where the souls of good people and the children crying in the dead end of the road are seen.

City

When I see the sea,
I feel the love and heart of God.
Go to a park in the city where no one,
when I look at the streets of the city
of full of light,
the tears of the Lord come to my mind.
I miss a warm hearted person here.
Everyone walks down the street.
When looking at their eyes,
I miss the joy of a person
who cares with warm smiles
and greetings.
When we look at the sky,
we feel God's infinite desire.
When the desire is raining and snowing
and reaching the ground,
the steps toward home are lighter.
One small flower on the roadside is the most
precious and beautiful.

Barren land

I looked at the empty nest of the park
where the rainy season of that year passed.
They knew their minds,
and they chased the clouds
without any hesitation.
The land of the city is invisible.
Even when the rainy season comes,
those who left without
being able to absorb the wet water
even in the midst of the coming
season resembled them.

Past times

There was an old drawer with a folded calendar. I accidentally opened the folded calendar while I was cleaning my desk. I saw a date in the middle of August as shown above on a torn calendar piece. Years later, I remember that time. It was dry and hot. And with a long drought, people were waiting for the rain. In a dry mountain in the western part, a forest fire continued for a month, and the flames continued to spread northward. I saw a simple note on the date. When will this drought end? But I am going through another drought right now. Like a pioneer in search of a land that does not dry, but I am still thinking of a time that does not change with a piece of the old calendar, I still find another way here. In our deepest mind, we have a calendar with a memorable date for anyone who has been folded for a long time.

Night View

To forget the loneliness on purpose,
I climb up a city high park overlooking
the city late at night.
The city lights from there
remind us of the decorations
of all kinds of confetti.
What color do I have in that light?
The little beasts of the park sleep
in their caves and
I hide in the lights and talk to the stars
with low sound.
When you are pure and passionate,
go to the beautifully embroidered place.
If all the moments of my life were like that,
I go there today to feel that I am not alone.

Puberty

When I walk along a small forest road, I meet a stepping bridge, and I feel I crossed a bigger bridge than a child's height. We waited for the age of adulthood in such a small, exciting little island on young minds, in a little island carved in a young mind. Now I am cherishing the time of the festive autumn day. We will soon have a warm winter here. I've never seen warm snow like this before. The joyful imagination that did not freeze the flowing water made me feel mature and joyful. Adulthood always waited for us in that little forest. With the blazing life in the woods and the wondrous winter stories and the distant sounds of the season of youth.

What silence

The bones of sound grow as deep as thought. We've always heard stories of countries that were never known to tired travelers from a distant country and told people. As the high peaks covered with ice caps became the hard bones of the mountains, the heavy silence that has covered so many of these old cities has always seemed like a revolution in front of the story. Are not you afraid? The hard buildings that do not shake and the heavy silence crouching down the corner, the cold blooded ones who are not disturbed by the story of man.

Crossing 1

We are strangers everywhere.
Standing at the intersection of the streets
occasionally would have made me feel
like I was standing in the backyard of
a garden where I did not grow old.
In old trees in the middle of the garden,
small birds that had just flown
in the forest nestled,
and the noise of the young children
became echoed in the small space.
I can not gaze in any direction
in a square space.
When I passed by the people,
I became a stranger and their greeting
and warm expression would become
nameless flowers and fragrance.
There, the fog did not disappear easily.
There was only the shape of a little person.

Mural of City

I saw an eagle mural that could not be attached
to the gray wall. It was a city. There were many
rainy and dry seasons, and there was a fantasy
world that could not be caught between people's
emotions and reality. I knew that the mighty
bird picture that could not move was moving the
viewer's heart. Then we were flying together.
I saw a city falling through the cracked clouds.
We could not forget those gazes that looked at us
from high up. When I looked at it for a long time,
the dried ground was revealed in the fleeting
time, and I had to hide in the murals and wait
for people to come back.

Crossing 2

The city expands along the maze.
At the end of that uncharted road,
the boundaries of what some people
are revolting about in life have given
birth to different boundaries,
and we have lost our way on the streets.
There was always only a heavy sadness
that could not be expressed in the graffiti
of a boy between the walls of dry buildings,
where the damp wind did not stop.
The city could not smell any earthy smell.
The people who went silently on the old chair
and the people who are looking for another way
in the labyrinth,
here are the times of rebellion
where everything is destroyed
and rebuilt by someone

Way

It is not going this way alone.
A man with a weak mind makes a difference
among people and disappears himself
with contention, jealousy, and hatred.
Always hiding and standing
in the dark night sky
for a moment standing alone lying
like a moon again,
the only place you go is a lonely land
where inexperienced people live.
Tolerance and forgiveness love
enriches our spirit
and makes us strong.
Let's go up to the mountain together.
Let's cross the sea with waves.
The days of poverty in life are a moment,
He who gazes on the invisible land
will never go this way alone;
he will always have the same springtime sun.

Dove of the city

All that is needed here is
the eye of the shorebirds
and the courage and honor of the eagle.
I always fly over the gray altar
and rest under the shade of a quiet building.
It will not disappear in a day.
You will have to look far.
Do not be afraid of the eyes
and of the clouds that are in front of you.
From a distance, when a siren sounds
more and more toward this place,
people awaken from the deep sleep one by one.
I need only the attentive eyes
and the courage not to scare the things
to be done on that day.
The city does not foreshadow the fog.
But we ought to find ourselves places resting on,

Festival

When they have a holiday,
their procession comes to look like a mallard
looking for a warm place with a long flock.
It resembles a horde of salmon
that once experienced the widest place
that goes back along a narrow,
shallow small river.
Children who are out of
parental hands resemble voices
that have become adults.
You should not forget
where you should be at once.
Prepare things that will be good
for your life and clean water for a soul,
and prepare for a warm winter.
Can you think of living without preparing a day?
The night sky is covered with
a green-colored dancing aurora
and will reach to a morning of excitement.
Now let's make a place to go back to adults
and find them again.
It will reveal it again with a bright lamp.

Neon

When I was a child,
there was a flying firefly in the green light
at night through the grass.
For a while, I had forgotten those small,
bright lights, so I met them in the city.
With wings that humbly light the darkness,
they were now resembling strange cities.
If it had not been with the moonlight,
it would have been a story that
could not be read in our faded bookmarks,
but the dreamy boy was alive again.
Look!
Everyone in front of
the light of the city's fireflies
in all the colors will be dreamy children.
One morning as we wake up from a long sleep,
will we make this city be prosperous?

Having met a friend of the poor

Having met a friend of
the poor here in the city,
there will be a pleasant meeting
in the place where
I promised to become a new person.
I prepare good clothes, food, and music.
I took off my ragged clothes
and just changed to new, clean
and shiny clothes,
and I stood where everyone's eyes stay.
Let us warm our hearts and greetings
and give our little garden to those who
have no place to lean on.
Love is beautiful,
and your shoulders are really warm.
Let us go to the place we promised
on the first train to arrive at this terminal station.
There will be waiting for a real friend of the poor,

PART 3

Hometown

There was always a small mountain
and a creek no matter how small a town.
How wide was the narrow path at that time?
Our hearts and minds have grown,
and now we have learned to live together
with everything around us.
Your little gaze resembles your home
where you want so much.
I hope that the warm sunshine of the midday
will also stay in places like lonely wetlands.
Even in the smallest town,
there is the nostalgia
and conversation of our neighbors,
so when we stop at our feet,
we lay down our heavy burdens,

Some loneliness

I see people sitting on park benches
with familiar names that any city knows.
No one speaks to them
They stay in the lake
in front of the park for a while
They see the crowd of migratory birds
disappear somewhere.
The mind is not quiet.
Anxiety does not leave.
I see Blue Jay from a strange place.
There is a smile on people's faces.
Wherever the tranquility could be found,
there was no building in the city
that built the foundation deep
in the ground.
I did not find the place to lean on
in any family members who went out together.
People who lose parks are always anxious.
We must hold on to the mind
that is moving away.
Before the direction cannot be measured
where a wind will come and head for.

Plaza

Go to the plaza together
before the night dew covering upon there.
I want to choose the widest
and most visible place there
and invite my friends.
At night we talked about a small revolution
and put it into practice.
Now that morning, the world will be changed.
Lift a small candle in your hand.
Wherever candlelight falls,
our sorrows disappear
and our hearts will be joined together to become
a land that anyone in this square can bear.
The old clown is soon to go their home
and sing a song of a revolution
that dances to the music at night.
Before the night dew falls,
let us go to the lighted square.

The altar

There must be a distinguished altar here.
I have to invite the altar to a holy ritual
with a clean smell to the corner of the city.
There is no creature that breathes
where the border collapses.
We have to wait in the highest place.
Whether it is an altar that everyone knows
or a stranger in the arms of persons,
we must live the distinction
between the clean and the unclean.
When we see the ivy grass that grows
among the building forests
where the sun rises and falls,
I feel like we should be like that.
It is not far from the boundaries
that block the boundaries from themselves.
Now if you hold your hand and hold it all,
it will soon become an altar.
It becomes an altar without boundaries.

Compass

Find the map and mark it,
again and again, to avoid getting lost.
Find out the timetable
and route in advance
to see how many buses I should take.
Many people are already
waiting for the bus stop.
The long procession of people standing
in a line resembles a migratory bird
that tries to make a long line toward
a warm sunny place.
People with wings bent on one side see.
As there is no sanctuary anywhere,
I opened the compass
in place and led them.
People laughed at me.
But I could not respond
to their warm response.
The station was soaked
with sudden clouds of rain
and showers,
but not many people entered the platform
in order to avoid the rain.

Cats on the street

At midnight, the last trembling
of the old bulb was visible.
Underneath the pole was an unfinished task
that followed the memories of the horn.
We can not find anyone who has met
in any way and has come so far.
The last breath in the bright moonlight
and their attachment to life became
a rite for them to pass.
We want to find answers to
these unfinished tasks when
we seeing a small mound in the city
and a passage on this street
that leads deep into the ground.
They look like them.
Maybe they should be there as midnight,
they are seen in the shadows of the stars.

Wind

If you are in the center of the wind,
you can determine the direction of the wind.
It seemed that the children
who moved the kites in a winter field
knew the principle.
So they are great.
If you do not stand in the center of the wind,
you can not go back up the path.
It is not unfamiliar to us to talk about the people
who went to the tree to find
kites hanging between branches.
I would rather have told the people
who choose the last breath
under a shabby building in the city today
that I can live without wind in the wind,
watching the crows' moving away,

Subway Station

The sidewalk that people walked
through was worn out.
Numerous of their sweaty harvests were
so familiar to small animals
that lived in the corner of a street.
Everything that lives here
does not leave deep, dark traces.
Only horrifying indifferent expressions
were inherited to later generations.
Today we are looking for a way
to find the remnants of racial issues
that nobody likes.
The train station alarm clock was always
pointing to noon.
Many people were living in a firm belief
that the time would not be wrong,
and we were waiting for a train
that would not come with an unchanging look.

A buddy

Someday you'll find it here.
The traces of children
who stayed for a long time.
At that time, old things and things
that are already broken
are going to be renewed again.
Maybe we'll come to the world for a while.
The word 'if' would be unfamiliar
to some street flowers.
Today I am supposed to meet someone here.
Even if he does not come looking for me,
all the disappearing traces
will still be a precious guest to me.
It will be a whisper to hear even silence
in this space where we are staying.
You started dreaming my little children
in dreams.

Deep

Deep rivers are calm.
The birds of height know well
the flow of the wind.
I want people living here
to be like them.
It is a life that imitates man,
as we also have a desire for hope
when we meet people
who have sought calm
and peace of mind.
As the change of the environment
leads to rather a matureness,
the survivors should not stay in one place.
Do not change it everywhere.
Every time we see the rising sun
and the moonlight shining brightly at night.

Gap

If we take a breath on the ground with a small gap in the asphalt, we will probably be just such a small creature. As soon as all the sleep on the ground flees, this is always a new morning sunshine. I saw the small roots of the ivy that would overtake the years with the crevices of red brick buildings over a hundred years old, which would someday make a loud noise. Everyone who breathes here will be wrapped around the body and all things bent will probably return to their place. On the day when all the sadness on earth disappears, this place becomes an altar that no one can rebel against. Are you seeing adults and children grow one by one in that gap?

I asked on the road.

Nobody knows where the end of the road is when you see the long stretch of road. The people here seemed like it, as a kite hanging on a high branch and no longer able to fly. Soon, the traces we stayed in will also be erased. Those who went to the ends of the earth do not reach there. I still can not find a place to go, the streets are transformed into one night, and the elderly people gazing at the sky sitting on the chair of the park will someday disappear. We are standing right in the middle of the familiar road as the place that no one else has settled in time and has not lived is not the end.

City Aurora

Every night I saw
the guests of joy coming back
as if they spread their splendid hem.
They hold their hands with
unbending intimacy with a fearless face,
old things are renewed,
dark things are turned into light.
Here you can see the polar festival.
Those who hold each other's hands
and cross the street with candles and prayers.
I see that burning scent.
It climbs into the night sky
and kisses with the stars.
surprising.
We also knew that there was such enthusiasm
for youth and a firm commitment to
a fervent revolution.
It was here at the end of the continent,
where the mother was,
and where the laughs
and stories of the brethren sprang up.
Very closely.

Late Fall

It was always crowded with those who tried to experience the rebellion without any reason. Sidewalk block Dandelion seeds broke through cracks and climbed up to the ground and stood out. So without counting the discipline of countless people, they sang resistance songs in front of the collapsed order. When is the yellow fallen leaf falling all over here and hiding the ugly look? Tonight, lovers gather together in the autumn night, listening to the song of the cricket. We were not lonely. It is because we still have time to dream of happiness because we can rebel against someone and live our lives by playing one instrument at our own discretion.

Trace

The memories of the dead men
lying in front of an old churchyard,
the memories of their survivors who left
their traces quietly in the land without names,
the scattered leaves wet with late autumn foliage,
Only the traces keeps its place.
We see a long life there.
Is it time for us to go now?
The fog starts to dawn.
Soon a warm sun will come in here. The silent
promises left on the stone, their traces of
lightly returning to the private
land after a short journey,

Empty house

All the people have left empty house
The sound of rain falling on eaves,
resembling the sobs of missing someone.
I saw a long procession of people passing
through the city in time for the first train
of the day and a flock of geese flying south.
The rain has not soaked their bodies,
and it cannot catch their feet.
Only compassion for those who have gone astray
is left in the empty house.
The pictures of children who want to be painted
on the wallpaper, old crepe sculptures
without the owner,
in which our dreams have to wait for tomorrow
with the broken alarm clock that has stopped.
When there is a vacant house left by people,
we have to go there.
For those who travel a long way,

Playground

The corner of the playground
where the snow did not accumulate
was the place where the children's laughter
and footsteps remained,
and their heat always brought sunshine.
In the snowstorm, we sit there
and tell the memories of last summer.
We knew. That they did not lose their innocence
always had a desire for them in their hearts.
Through the hands of the children,
the little stone sculptures of the playground
become pebbles of the person's hand
and the nostalgia with the sound of
a small wave on a beach.
When we enter the school's playground,
the good deep heart that we have forgotten is
calling us.

Falling Frost

One late frost day,
I saw the lasting leaves
on the poplar trees above the roads.
That last affair tells stories of people
who have passed through the streets.
We must hear our bronze horses' crying
and the sound of rings.
It was our life to come for a while,
but the land that we are standing on
will never dry because of the breeze of
the frost that will be forgotten.
The sea is constantly buried
in the deep water, the soft sand to the beach,
and everything that has been lost is reborn
on the trail of a leaf that has fallen off a soft
branch.
Then I knew. The late frost was so warm.

Wall Graffiti

In the space where people live,
always look at the shapes of
the sadness being raised,
the smiles that cry over there.
There is always only one piece of cloud
that holds the humidity to dominate the space.
We have forgotten the days of youth.
Waiting for the future nihilism that will not
come.
The murals painted on old walls of the city's
quiet
and nobody will visit it.
Many cats pass the front of us
as they smell the genitals.
So sorrow was tamed and we were waiting
for a broken future in a wall graffiti painting.

if a spirited youth didn't find you,
we would be more peaceful
and we would creatively write and paint on
all of beautiful things.

"they don't have any expectation for dreaming."

moi would be honored
for continued a long life,
but the sense of loss should be left behind
remembering your return to the spaces.

it's old, but I always feel new when I look at the space.
I hope that our pure feelings are lost.
we must leave behind the pure wills of those who remain here,
and the memories we will miss at some point in the future.

I have feelings, and love them all.
that is the reason why I live here.

we extend thanks to them,
some lifelong, some new.
we will survive at last.

they have a very unfavorable view of the place.
the land that has been steadily maintained
for decades is unpredictable.
the eyes that looked at the collapsed house resembled
the eyes of a pure boy who lost his parents and wandered.
there was no response to his desperate request.
perhaps you were hoping for a sincere recovery in it.

when you first appeared in this world,
it always seemed like a creative mania
to make anything.
it seemed you could do
whatever you wanted.
but we stand in a beautiful valley
where you can not stand.

they have beautiful words and areas
that are not already in this world.
so maybe
we could not have expected optimism in the future.

it may be in transition.
I could not find any news
of the daily newspaper
about the difficult process or
the death of a friendly person
who left the world.

The city is beautiful and everything is alive in it. Life is like a marsh that hasn't always been dry, and there will always be good breath and good people,

From Yongjea John Han

www.ingramcontent.com/pod-product-compliance
Lightning Source LLC
Chambersburg PA
CBHW032130090426
42743CB00007B/540